LIFE IN THE SPECIAL FORCES

LIFE AS A PARARESCUE SPECIALIST

by Cynthia Kennedy Henzel

BrightPoint Press

San Diego, CA

© 2024 BrightPoint Press
an imprint of ReferencePoint Press, Inc.
Printed in the United States

For more information, contact:
BrightPoint Press
PO Box 27779
San Diego, CA 92198
www.BrightPointPress.com

ALL RIGHTS RESERVED.

No part of this work covered by the copyright hereon may be reproduced or used in any form or by any means—graphic, electronic, or mechanical, including photocopying, recording, taping, web distribution, or information storage retrieval systems—without the written permission of the publisher.

LIBRARY OF CONGRESS CATALOGING-IN-PUBLICATION DATA

Names: Henzel, Cynthia Kennedy, 1954– author.
Title: Life as a pararescue specialist / Cynthia Kennedy Henzel.
Description: San Diego, CA: BrightPoint, [2024] | Series: Life in the special forces | Includes bibliographical references and index. | Audience: Grades 7–9
Identifiers: LCCN 2023036986 (print) | LCCN 2023036987 (eBook) | ISBN 9781678207441 (hardcover) | ISBN 9781678207458 (eBook)
Subjects: LCSH: United States. Air Force--Search and rescue operations--Juvenile literature. | Special forces (Military science)--Juvenile literature. | CYAC: Special forces (Military science)
Classification: LCC UG633 .H398 2024 (print) | LCC UG633 (eBook) | DDC 358.4--dc23/eng/20230804
LC record available at https://lccn.loc.gov/2023036986
LC eBook record available at https://lccn.loc.gov/2023036987

CONTENTS

AT A GLANCE	4
INTRODUCTION PLANE DOWN!	6
CHAPTER ONE SUPERMAN SCHOOL	12
CHAPTER TWO EQUIPMENT AND VEHICLES	24
CHAPTER THREE IT TAKES A TEAM	34
CHAPTER FOUR QUIET HEROES	46
Glossary	58
Source Notes	59
For Further Research	60
Index	62
Image Credits	63
About the Author	64

AT A GLANCE

- Pararescue specialists, also known as PJs, are part of the US Air Force's special operations forces.

- The PJs' primary mission is to rescue military members who find themselves in dangerous situations. They may rescue troops who are at risk of being captured by enemy forces.

- PJs train to parachute into water or onto land for rescues.

- These troops are trained to scuba dive for rescues or insertions into some combat zones.

- PJs are trained in Survival, Evasion, Resistance, Escape (SERE) in case they are captured.

- They learn combat skills and often fight alongside other special operations units, such as US Navy SEALs.

- PJs receive medical training so they can treat wounded troops in the field.

- Pararescue specialists receive some of the longest instruction among the military's special forces. They train for approximately 2 years.

- PJs often rescue civilians during national disasters or emergencies.

INTRODUCTION

PLANE DOWN!

Sergeant Ross hears the engines roar as the plane approaches the jump zone. Somewhere in the ocean below is a downed aircraft. The pararescue specialists, also known as PJs, don't know if the two airmen on the plane are injured or if enemy boats are nearby.

Cold air blasts in as a large door on the back of the plane opens. The team leader, or jumpmaster, sees nothing but darkness below him. Sunrise isn't due for another 30 minutes. But the airmen need help now. Ross and the other PJs stand up. They clip lines attached to their parachutes to a steel cable overhead. A red light by the door turns green.

Pararescue specialists must perform their missions whenever their help is needed. This sometimes means parachuting in the dark.

Pararescue specialists are trained to deliver medical treatment wherever an emergency takes place.

"Go!" the jumpmaster yells before jumping out the door. The others follow. One by one, their parachutes open.

They drift downward and unclip their parachutes just before hitting the water.

Ross swims toward a bright light. It is on a crate that the team dropped from the plane before the PJs jumped. Ross helps unpack and inflate the rubber raft inside. Another PJ starts the raft's engine. Soon, the team arrives at the downed plane.

Ross climbs onto the wreckage. One man's arm is bleeding. PJs help him into the raft and begin treatment. The pilot is still pinned in the plane. Ross pulls a power saw from his backpack. He cuts the metal that is trapping the pilot as the plane sinks. The pilot's leg is broken. Ross puts a splint on the leg so it cannot move. The team lifts the pilot out. Other PJs keep a lookout for enemy boats and call headquarters. They wait for the rescue boat to arrive.

THAT OTHERS MAY LIVE

Pararescue specialists are members of Air Force Special Warfare. They are trained to rescue other military members who are in danger. PJs also rescue civilians when necessary.

PJs learn to parachute so they can reach people quickly. They learn to scuba dive for water rescues. Using their medical training, they treat people with serious injuries until they can be transported to a hospital. PJs, often called guardian angels in the military, risk their lives by going into dangerous places to help others. This special force's motto is "These Things We Do, That Others May Live."

Pararescue specialists are trained to reach fellow military members or civilians in any type of environment.

1

SUPERMAN SCHOOL

Training to become a PJ is often called going to Superman school. The 2-year training is among the longest of any special forces. Because it is so difficult, only about 20 percent of those who begin PJ training finish it. PJ Eric P. Hansen knows his work is difficult. But he thinks the people he rescues are doing more important work.

He says, "We do missions because they do missions a lot greater than ours."[1]

Training begins with physical fitness work. Candidates swim, run, lift weights, and complete obstacle courses. This 8-week course teaches medical and dive vocabulary too.

Strong swimming skills are essential for pararescue specialists. Saving people in the water is a big part of their job.

Candidates who pass the physical fitness test then spend 7 weeks at the Special Warfare Preparatory Course at Lackland Air Force Base in Texas. They then spend 4 weeks completing the Special Warfare Assessment and Selection Course. This physical training takes place under stressful conditions, such as lack of sleep. This helps the military decide who is physically and mentally ready for continued PJ training.

AIR FORCE COMBAT DIVE SCHOOL

Successful candidates move on to a pre-dive school. This provides them with the physical and mental training to work as a diver. Pararescue specialist Ivan Ruiz explains, "Take the air away from somebody, and you really see how they react under stress. The individual needs to complete a given task before they come back up for air. If they do one thing wrong, they get stressed out and things start to snowball. You can imagine what happens after that."[2]

The next step is the Air Force Combat Dive School in Florida. It is one of the military's hardest courses. One of the more difficult diving exercises is drownproofing.

AIR FORCE COMBAT DIVE COURSE

The Air Force Combat Dive Course began in 2006 in Panama City, Florida. Before then, PJ candidates trained with the Army at its combat dive facility. With its own facility, the Air Force focuses on the types of diving PJs perform, such as advanced rescue diving.

The goal of drownproofing is to teach pararescue specialists how to stay alive if they become trapped in water.

With hands and feet tied, the swimmer moves from the pool's bottom to the water's surface. This action is repeated for 5 minutes in 10 feet (3 m) of water.

This test requires enormous self-control. If swimmers gulp too much air, they sink too slowly to the bottom. They will use up their air too quickly. If they push off the bottom too hard, they break their ties and are disqualified. While still tied, swimmers then float on the water's surface for 2 minutes. This is followed by a 100-yard (91-m) swim. Next, the swimmers do a front and a back flip underwater and pick up a face mask from the bottom of the pool with their teeth. Finally, they do five more bobs while holding the face mask in their teeth.

Combat dive school teaches scuba diving. Candidates also learn to use inflatable boats and diver propulsion devices. These are small, open submarines that carry two divers. In addition, candidates practice tactics for going into a combat zone and for **navigation**.

SKYDIVING

Basic training in static line parachuting takes place at Airborne School at Fort Benning, Georgia. In static line jumping, a cable runs from the jumper's chute to the plane. As jumpers leave the plane, their weight pulls the cable to open the chute. At first, they practice by jumping off a 250-foot (76.2-m) tower. Finally, they jump from an airplane at 1,250 feet (381 m).

It is common for students to be afraid. Instructor Robert Nicoson says, "They don't lose their fear of heights, but they get it out of their head. I try to tell them that I'm scared to death of heights, and I've been

Static line jumping is safer than other methods of parachuting for people new to jumping. For this reason, it is the first type of parachuting that pararescue specialists are taught.

jumping for 10 years. I try to keep it in their mind that we're all scared."[3]

When pararescue specialists perform free-fall jumps, they fall as fast as 125 miles per hour (201 kmh) before opening their chutes.

Next, the Military Freefall Course in Yuma, Arizona, teaches free-fall skydiving. Free-fall skydiving means jumping from the plane and then falling through the air before opening the parachute. The parachutists open their own chutes when they are ready.

PJ candidates travel to Fairchild Air Force Base in Washington State for the Survival, Evasion, Resistance, Escape (SERE) Course. SERE teaches survival in isolated areas until help arrives. PJs must avoid capture by enemies and know what to do if they are captured.

COMBAT AND MEDICINE

Back at Lackland Air Force Base, medical training comes in the Modernized Pararescue Provider Program. This training takes approximately 39 weeks. PJs are certified as emergency medical technicians (EMTs) and paramedics. In addition, they learn how to care for patients while waiting for help. PJs must be prepared for chemical, biological, radiation, or nuclear contamination.

Students attend combat training at Kirtland Air Force Base in New Mexico. Many missions require PJs to secure an area as part of a rescue. This training teaches them tactics for such assignments. It also teaches students combat and weaponry skills.

After completing all courses, students graduate. PJs wear a deep maroon beret. The blood-red color is a symbol of the sacrifices made by fellow PJs and their dedication to the duty of saving others.

MINIMUM AND RECOMMENDED SCORES FOR PJ CANDIDATES

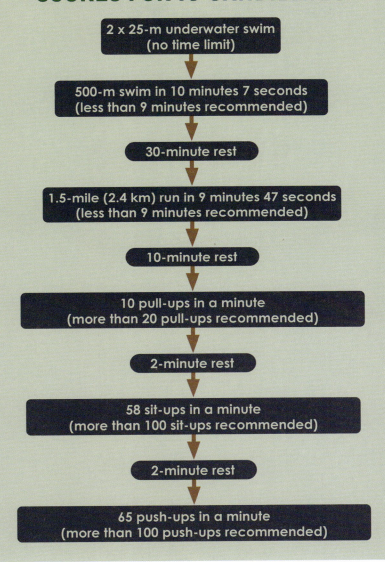

These are minimum scores in fitness to get into the PJ program. But to be successful, candidates must strive to do better than the minimum.

2
EQUIPMENT AND VEHICLES

Pararescue specialists must carry everything they might need for a rescue when they jump from a plane. Former PJ Brian Kimber says, "Being a PJ to me meant primarily helping people who found themselves in trouble. And to do that, you had to be the man with the plan; the guy who was prepared to go anywhere on earth, anytime, and be able to help someone."[4] PJs may rescue someone from under a collapsed building. The next rescue may be a person trapped in an icy **crevasse**. When jumping into water or scuba diving, PJs may carry up to 170 pounds (77 kg) of equipment.

The equipment pararescue specialists need depends on the mission. But common items include body armor, weapons, radios, and night-vision goggles.

PJs use several types of parachutes for jumps. Static line jumps are performed at 15,000 feet (4,572 m) or lower. The parachute used is the T-11 Advanced Tactical Parachute System. It comes with a harness, a square-shaped main parachute, and a reserve parachute. The design creates less shock on opening than older parachutes. It also provides a slower descent speed, which makes landing safer.

During High Altitude/High Opening (HAHO) free-fall jumps, PJs may jump from 30,000 feet (9,144 m). This is approximately where commercial airplanes fly. They pull a **rip cord** to open their chutes and steer to a specific point up to 40 miles (64 km) away. This allows jumpers to enter places where the plane cannot fly, such as over international borders.

Pararescue specialists may need to wear an oxygen mask for certain jumps. The higher the jump, the less oxygen there is in the air.

HAHO jumpers use ram-air parachutes. These are long and rectangular. They have two layers of fabric that form cells between the layers. The cells inflate during the descent. These chutes let the PJ control the speed and direction during the ride down.

There is little oxygen at high altitudes. PJs wear special helmets to protect their ears and eyes. They breathe from oxygen bottles to avoid passing out.

During High Altitude/Low Opening (HALO) jumps, PJs free-fall to a low altitude, sometimes as low as 800 feet (244 m). They then open their parachutes. Opening the parachutes late in the jump keeps enemies from spotting the PJs.

PJs use different equipment for the two types of scuba diving they perform. Traditional scuba equipment includes tanks of air, which PJs carry on their backs. They breathe air from the tanks and release carbon dioxide as bubbles that float to the water's surface. But bubbles can give away a diver's location. Tankless diving does not produce bubbles. Instead, the system recycles the gases from breathing.

SAFETY EQUIPMENT

The Battlefield Air Targeting Man-Aided Knowledge (BATMAN) program tests technology that PJs use to do their jobs better. BATMAN takes place at the Air

FIRST PARACHUTE RESCUE

In 1943, flight surgeon Colonel Don Fleckinger, with medics Sergeant Richard Passey and Corporal William MacKenzie, made the first pararescue. They parachuted from a search plane to rescue twenty-one men. The men had bailed out of a damaged C-46 Commando aircraft into a remote jungle near the China-Burma border. With help from local people, the rescuers cared for the wounded for nearly a month until help arrived.

Force Research Laboratory. One of the tools the program developed is the Battlefield Airmen Trauma Distributed Observation Kit (BATDOK). For a long time, pararescue specialists could treat patients only one-to-one. But this kit allows them to treat multiple patients simultaneously. A smartphone collects information such as blood pressure and heart rate from monitors on the patients. BATDOK then records and sends out the information.

To keep PJs safe, BATMAN tested the flashing indicator of swimmer's health (FISH) monitor. The monitor measures oxygen levels in the blood while a swimmer is underwater. It flashes to alert the swimmer if oxygen dips too low. Too little oxygen can cause a swimmer to black out and drown.

The BATDOK performs a variety of helpful tasks. They include identifying patients' exact locations for pickup and adding data to patients' health records in real time.

The spatial proximity under-canopy reporting sensor (SPURS) is worn on a jumper's foot. It tells a parachutist the distance to the ground. This tool helps prevent injuries, especially during night jumps.

The GARC is propelled by jets instead of propeller blades. This design prevents the watercraft from injuring victims in the water.

VEHICLES

Pararescue specialists use different vehicles for different missions. One assignment may require an ATV. Another might require a snowmobile. The Guardian Angel Air-Deployable Rescue Vehicle (GAARV) is a small pickup truck made to be carried by an airplane or helicopter. It allows PJs to be dropped off outside the range of enemy anti-aircraft weapons. The PJs can then drive to the area where they are needed. The GAARV is designed to carry twice its own weight and can travel at speeds up to 100 miles per hour (161 kmh).

For water rescues, PJs may use the Guardian Angel Rescue Craft (GARC). It is designed to transport several people. The craft is powered by water jets. This means there is no propeller that could injure people in the water.

Pararescue teams often use the C-130 Hercules four-engine turboprop plane for drops. However, some pararescue units use the C-17 Globemaster III aircraft. This plane is designed for long-range missions. It is faster and can carry two rescue helicopters.

3

IT TAKES A TEAM

The work a pararescue team performs depends on its type. A rescue **squadron** (RQS) performs personnel recovery. This type of team is made up of PJs, combat rescue officers, and SERE specialists. The PJs perform the rescue missions, and combat rescue officers oversee the team. SERE specialists analyze the ground conditions where the recovery will take place.

Combat rescue officers are commissioned officers in the Air Force.

Some pararescue teams perform search and rescue missions after natural disasters, such as hurricanes.

Commissioned officers have college degrees and have attended Officer Training School. Their training is similar to a PJ's. But combat rescue officers don't go through medical training. Instead, they train to organize and coordinate operations. They may deploy with PJs or with a special tactics team to coordinate rescues on the ground. A combat rescue officer's job is to enable others to save lives.

PJs AND NASA

On March 17, 1966, the Gemini 8 space flight made an emergency landing in the Pacific Ocean. NASA called the pararescue specialists. Three PJs parachuted in. Within 20 minutes, they stabilized the capsule. The PJs stayed with the two-man crew until a Navy ship arrived 3 hours later.

Rescue squadrons usually deploy as a team using HH-60 helicopters or C-130 airplanes. They often do civil search and rescue. This means they respond to floods, hurricanes, and other disasters to save civilians. They may work with the Federal Emergency Management Agency (FEMA), the United States Agency for International Development (USAID), or rescue organizations. Barry D. Smith is an instructor at the Regional Emergency Medical Services Authority in Reno, Nevada. He says, "US civilian authorities are turning to the military more and more for local and regional emergencies. As the role of the PJ shifts, they will adjust their training, skills, and equipment to match the challenges."[5]

Hurricane Michael struck Florida in October 2018. Pararescue specialists in New York packed their search and rescue gear to help with the natural disaster.

SPECIAL TACTICS SQUADRONS

A special tactics squadron (STS) is part of strike and recovery missions. These combat missions often recover military personnel. But they may also rescue civilians. Along with PJs, an STS mission has combat control specialists, special **reconnaissance** tactical air control specialists, and special tactics officers. Sometimes, multiple PJs deploy together. In other cases, individual PJs may join missions with other special operations forces, such as Navy SEALs or Green Berets.

Air support for the STS includes pilots and crews of a variety of aircraft. Other support personnel include people who pack parachutes and prepare other equipment.

Rescuing fellow military personnel is a big part of a pararescue specialist's job. This often means entering dangerous combat environments.

Master Sergeant Cody Inman says, "For every pararescueman or combat rescue officer . . . there's probably seven to ten support personnel behind them."[6]

The majority of PJs are active-duty service members in the Air Force. This means that the Air Force is their full-time job. These PJs often move every few years to different teams. Active-duty teams are located in the United States and overseas.

Other PJs are part of five Air National Guard units. They may be full-time or part-time. Part-time National Guard members train one weekend each month and for an additional 2 weeks each year. They may be called up for full-time service when they are needed. National Guard PJs stay in one location rather than moving from place to place. Part-time PJs often have other jobs or go to school while working as a PJ.

SPECIAL TEAMS

All pararescue specialists are trained in a variety of tasks. But most PJs have developed some skills more than others. A well-balanced PJ team has members with different specialties. Some PJ teams specialize in specific types of rescues such as mountain, arctic, or diving. The specialty teams are located where those skills are most needed.

The RQS California National Guard PJ team is known for its parachuting ability. When boats get in trouble at sea, beyond the distance where the Coast Guard operates, PJs come to their aid.

Aircrew flight equipment specialists inspect, maintain, and pack parachutes for pararescue specialists.

The PJs can parachute anywhere in the Pacific Ocean. They can aid sick or injured passengers until help arrives.

The New York team is known for its medical skills. These PJs were among the first responders to the World Trade Center after the terrorist attacks on September 11, 2001. The Alaska Air National Guard PJ

Pararescue specialists trained for mountain rescues are often sent to help injured hikers in remote areas, such as Alaska.

team is known for its medical and mountain skills. They are also the busiest RQS. They average one rescue per week, covering everything from lost hikers to bear attacks.

Another team at Patrick Air Force Base in Florida works with NASA. In 2019, NASA announced plans to send astronauts on a moon landing mission. Pararescue specialists have a plan to help these astronauts return to Earth. In this plan, the PJs would have a plane and two helicopters ready to go in case of an emergency landing. They would parachute to the splashdown site and use an inflatable ring to hold up the space capsule. They would then enter the capsule and provide medical aid. Finally, they would get the astronauts out of the capsule and into a raft to await air or sea transport.

4
QUIET HEROES

Pararescue specialists are not as well-known as Navy SEALs or Green Berets. But PJs are the most highly decorated unit in the Air Force. One PJ won a Congressional Medal of Honor, the United States' highest military award for **valor**. Twenty-two enlisted members of the Air Force have received the Air Force Cross, the second-highest honor. Twelve of them were PJs. PJs have won 105 Silver Stars, the third-highest award.

PJs played a critical role in the 1993 Battle of Mogadishu in Somalia. They were part of special forces mission Task Force Ranger. The task was to hunt down

Fellow Air Force members honor the life of Senior Airman Jason Cunningham. The pararescue specialist was killed while saving the lives of ten other people.

Somali warlord Mohamed Farrah Aidid. The warlord and his men had killed United Nations aid workers and stolen food from starving refugees.

US special forces successfully captured twenty-four of Aidid's men. But the enemy shot down a US military Black Hawk helicopter. The PJs rushed to the crash site with the Combat Search and Rescue team. PJs Scott Fales and Timothy Wilkinson dropped from ropes as their helicopter hovered over the crash site. They were in the middle of a firefight. Fales was wounded. But the PJs got the wounded Rangers out of the downed helicopter while using their rifles to hold off the enemy. They dragged the Rangers into an empty house for protection. They then held off the enemy until the next morning when help arrived.

PJ Scott Fales received the Silver Star and the Purple Heart for his work as a pararescue specialist in 1993. Nineteen years later, Fales (right) was given the Bull Simons lifetime achievement award for his military service.

For his actions, Wilkinson received the Air Force Cross. Fales received the Silver Star and Purple Heart. The Purple Heart is given to military members who are wounded or killed by enemy action.

In 2018, PJ Gavin Fisher was part of a convoy in Afghanistan when the Taliban attacked. He was struck by **shrapnel**. Still, he managed to move his vehicle out of danger. While under fire, he treated two badly injured soldiers. He then kept them stable until an evacuation team arrived.

MEDAL OF HONOR

PJ William H. Pitsenbarger received the Medal of Honor for saving the lives of soldiers during the Vietnam War. He was killed during a battle as he evacuated the wounded. Pitsenbarger was awarded the Medal of Honor posthumously for his bravery. This means after his death.

General CQ Brown Jr. presented the Silver Star Medal certificate to Technical Sergeant Gavin Fisher (right) in 2019.

Fisher did not stop there. He stayed in the fight, which included a second ambush. Fisher treated five more wounded. He then made his way through 246 feet (75 m) of machine-gun fire to treat another

In 2005, pararescue specialists rescued civilians from the floodwaters of Hurricane Katrina. They rescued babies, elderly people, and even dogs.

five wounded. Fisher was badly wounded by a grenade. But he fired his machine gun until the team was safe. When the attack was over, Fisher had saved the lives of ten US soldiers. He also helped evacuate twenty wounded soldiers and killed 118 Taliban fighters. Fisher later received the Silver Star.

NON-MILITARY RESCUE WORK

In August 2005, Hurricane Katrina struck New Orleans, Louisiana. Amid wind and debris, PJs **rappelled** from helicopters to rescue people from the floodwaters. Some PJs had to cut holes in roofs to rescue people trapped in attics. PJ Greggory Plasch says, "Being in my own country and rescuing American citizens had a big impact on me. We're set up for combat rescue. That means the people we pick up are usually (injured but otherwise) healthy people. But with Katrina, it ran the whole **gamut**—from infants to elderly. That part was pretty intense."[7] PJs helped save nearly 3,000 people. It was the largest rescue in Air Force history.

In 2018, PJs helped rescue a boys soccer team from a flooded cave in Thailand. The twelve boys ranged in age from 11 to 16. The players were trapped with their coach in an air pocket about 2 miles (3.2 km) inside the cave. Technical Sergeant Ken O'Brien traveled 550 yards (500 m) into the flooded tunnel. He spent 9 days in the cave providing medical care before divers brought the boys and the coach out.

Pararescue specialists don't make the news as much as some other US special forces. But they are always ready to put themselves in danger for the sake of saving others.

Helicopters often transport pararescue specialists both to and from their missions.

MAKING A DIFFERENCE

Personnel recovery is an important part of the Air Force's mission. PJ training changes as military tactics change. Pararescue specialists were originally trained to rescue downed pilots. They helped numerous airmen who were shot down during the

Korean War (1950–1953) and the Vietnam War (1954–1975). But their mission changed after the Vietnam War.

Today, they often travel by helicopter to rescue special operations forces such as Army Green Berets or Navy SEALs. Since the September 11 attacks, PJs have performed about 12,000 life-saving missions. They captured or killed many enemies during these missions. In addition, they rescued more than 5,000 civilians.

Lieutenant Colonel Stephen Rush is a flight surgeon. He says, "There is literally only one organization in the world that trains to this level as rescue specialists, that can do this totality of rescue specialized operations, and it is an honor for me to support these guys. They are amazing human beings."[8]

GLOSSARY

crevasse

a large, deep crack in a glacier or the ground

gamut

a range including everything

navigation

the process of finding a path to something or somewhere, often using maps or instruments

rappelled

descended by moving down a rope

reconnaissance

the process of observing an area to look for enemies or strategic targets

rip cord

a cord that is pulled to open a parachute

shrapnel

fragments thrown by an explosion

squadron

a basic fighting unit in the Air Force

valor

having great courage, especially in a battle

SOURCE NOTES

CHAPTER ONE: SUPERMAN SCHOOL

1. Quoted in Jacqueline Palochiko, "Rindge Soldier Featured on *National Geographic* Series," *The Keene Sentinel*, February 20, 2013. www.sentinelsource.com.

2. Quoted in Mark Synnott, "Injured Behind Enemy Lines, This Guy Is Your Best Friend," *National Geographic*, April 18, 2016. www.nationalgeographic.com.

3. Quoted in Katie Lange, "Airborne School," *US Department of Defense*, June 9, 2016. www.defense.gov.

CHAPTER TWO: EQUIPMENT AND VEHICLES

4. Quoted in Joshua Skovlund, "What It Means to Be a US Air Force Pararescue Jumper, According to 3 PJs," *Coffee or Die*, October 14, 2019. https://coffeeordie.com.

CHAPTER THREE: IT TAKES A TEAM

5. Barry D. Smith, "Extreme Rescue," *EMS World*, n.d. www.hmpgloballearningnetwork.com.

6. Quoted in Balina O'Neal Dresel, "Air Guard Unite to Save 19 During Hurricane Relief Ops," *Air Force Special Warfare*, September 18, 2018. https://afspecialwarfare.com.

CHAPTER FOUR: QUIET HEROES

7. Quoted in Julie Ray, "'Guardian Angels' Swoop Down from Above to Save Lives," *Air Force Special Operations Command*, November 3, 2005. www.afsoc.af.mil.

8. Quoted in Sarah McKernan, "NY 106th Rescue Wing Airmen Played Role in Thai Cave Rescue," *Air National Guard*, September 23, 2022. www.ang.af.mil.

FOR FURTHER RESEARCH

BOOKS

John Hamilton, *United States Air Force*. Minneapolis, MN: Abdo, 2020.

Cynthia Kennedy Henzel, *Life as a Green Beret*. San Diego, CA: BrightPoint Press, 2024.

Christina Soontornvat, *All Thirteen: The Incredible Cave Rescue of the Thai Boys' Soccer Team*. Somerville, MA: Candlewick, 2020.

INTERNET SOURCES

Kevin Grange, "Air Force Pararescue Team Saves Sick Baby 1,000 Miles Out at Sea," *Journal of Emergency Medical Services*, February 28, 2017. www.jems.com.

"Rescue Operations Take Shape for Commercial Crew Program Astronauts," *NASA*, May 1, 2018. www.nasa.gov.

Mark Synnott, "Injured Behind Enemy Lines, This Guy Is Your Best Friend," *National Geographic*, August 18, 2016. www.nationalgeographic.com.

WEBSITES

Air Force Special Warfare Knowledge Portal
https://afspecialwarfare.com/afspecwar-overview/pararescue/

The Air Force Special Warfare Knowledge Portal includes information about the job and history of pararescue specialists.

Pararescue Foundation
www.pararescuefoundation.org

The Pararescue Foundation's mission is to preserve and support the US Air Force Pararescue community. The site includes information about upcoming events.

US Air Force: Enlisted Pararescue
www.airforce.com/careers/combat-and-warfare/special-warfare/pararescue

The US Air Force website has a step-by-step guide to the training for a pararescue specialist.

INDEX

Air National Guard units, 41, 43–44
air support, 39
awards, 46–47, 49–50

Battle of Mogadishu, 47–48

combat skills, 17–18, 22, 39, 54

diving, 10, 13, 14–15, 17, 18–21, 25, 28, 42, 54
drownproofing, 15–17

equipment, 24–31

Fales, Scott, 48, 49
Fisher, Gavin, 50–53
Fleckinger, Don, 29

graduation, 22

Hurricane Katrina, 53–54

Inman, Cody, 41

Kimber, Brian, 24–25
Korean War, 56–57

MacKenzie, William, 29
medical skills, 10, 13, 21–22, 29, 36, 43–45, 54
mental fitness, 14–15
minimum scores, 23
motto, 10

NASA rescues, 36, 45
Nicoson, Robert, 18–19

O'Brien, Ken, 54

parachutes, 7, 8–9, 20–21, 26, 27, 28, 39
Passey, Richard, 29
physical fitness, 13, 14
Pitsenbarger, William H., 50
Plasch, Greggory, 53–54

rescue squadrons, 34, 37, 42, 45
Ruiz, Ivan, 14–15
Rush, Stephen, 57

skydiving, 18–21, 29, 36, 42–43, 45
special teams, 42–45
swimming, 9, 13, 16, 17, 23, 30

Thailand cave rescue, 54
training, 10, 12–23, 36, 37, 41, 42, 56, 57

vehicles, 32–33
Vietnam War, 56–57

weapons, 22
Wilkinson, Timothy, 48–49

IMAGE CREDITS

Cover: © Airman 1st Class Jacob Stephens/US Air Force/DVIDS
5: © Tech. Sgt. Larry Reid Jr./US Air Force/DVIDS
7: © Tech Sgt. Chris Hibben/US Air Force/DVIDS
8: © Airman 1st Class Daniel Hughes/DVIDS
11: © Senior Airman Zachary Rufus/US Air Force/DVIDS
13: © Staff Sgt. Jonathan Snyder/DVIDS
16: © Senior Airman Ryan Conroy/US Air Force/DVIDS
19: © Master Sgt. Russ Scalf/US Air Force/DVIDS
20: © Tech. Sgt. Daniel Asselta/US Air Force/DVIDS
23: © Red Line Editorial
25: © CGC Morgenthau/US Coast Guard/DVIDS
27: © Airman 1st Class Eugene Oliver/US Air Force/DVIDS
31: © Airman 1st Class Jose Miguel Tamondong/US Air Force/DVIDS
32: © Senior Airman John Linzmeier/US Air Force/DVIDS
35: © Senior Airman Moshe Paul/DVIDS
38: © Capt. Michael O'Hagan/US Air National Guard/DVIDS
40: © Staff Sgt. Eric Harris/US Air Force/DVIDS
43: © Tech. Sgt. Rachelle Coleman/US Air Force/DVIDS
44: © US Air Force/Senior Airman Andrew Lee/AirmanMagazine/Military Collection/Alamy
47: © Airman 1st Class Ericka Engblom/DVIDS
49: © Master Sgt. Larry Carpenter/DVIDS
51: © Airman 1st Class Bryan Guthrie/US Air Force/DVIDS
52: © Petty Officer 2nd Class Kyle Niemi/US Coast Guard/DVIDS
55: © Staff Sgt. Staci Miller/US Air Force/DVIDS
56: © Staff Sgt. Jonathan Snyder/US Air Force/DVIDS

ABOUT THE AUTHOR

Cynthia Kennedy Henzel has a BS in social studies education and an MS in geography. She has worked as a teacher-educator in many countries. Currently, she writes fiction and nonfiction books and develops education materials for social studies, history, science, and ELL students. She has written more than one hundred books and more than 150 stories for young people.